What is a Church ?

CAROLYN NYSTROM

Illustrated by
Wayne A. Hanna

MOODY PRESS
CHICAGO

ISBN: 0-8024-5998-6

Printed in the United States of America

3 4 5 6 7 Printing/DB/Year 87 86 85 84 83

Moody Press, a ministry of the Moody Bible Institute,
is designed for education, evangelization, and
edification. If we may assist you in knowing more about
Christ and the Christian life, please write us without
obligation: Moody Press, c/o MLM, Chicago, Illinois 60610.

What does your church look like?
Churches come in lots of different styles and
sizes.

Some are huge old buildings made of stone and glass. They took dozens of artists many years to build. These churches are called cathedrals.

Other churches are small simple buildings made of wood and shingles. A tall steeple helps everyone in a small town to find the church.

In cities, an empty store may be used as a church. People who live in the neighborhood can walk to church, and anyone walking down the sidewalk can easily stop in. This is called a storefront church.

In other neighborhoods, small groups
of people meet in the living room or basement
of a home. They sing and pray and study the
Bible just as people do in large buildings.
Children join with their parents. Those too
young to understand play quietly on
the floor. This is called a house church.

And here is my church. It is made of brick and concrete and wood. We started as a house church, but soon we had too many people to fit into a house. So we built this building. It is quite new. I come here every Sunday with Mom and Dad and Suzy and Seth. We come here at other times, too, for all kinds of special activities.

But a building, all by itself, is not a church. Only people make a church—all kinds of people.

There is a reason for that. When Jesus was on earth, He did all kinds of work.

Mark 1:40-42

With His hands He touched sick people and made them well.

John 14:8-11

With His mouth, He taught them to know God, His Father.

Mark 3:7-13

With His feet He walked to large cities, high mountains, and lonely deserts, so that He could help people in all those places.

Luke 24:27

With His mind He studied Scripture and explained it to everyone who listened.

John 21:1-14

Once Jesus cooked breakfast for His friends.

John 13:3-17

Another time He washed their feet.

John 10:17-18

Finally, He gave His whole body, let soldiers kill Him, so that God could forgive all the things that other people had done wrong.

John 17:18; Acts 1:1-9

But Jesus came back to life. He walked and talked with His friends for forty days. Then they watched Jesus go away into heaven. Before He left, Jesus told His friends that they must take His place on earth.

Colossians 1:18; Hebrews 10:24-25

No one person alone can do the work that Jesus began. That is why the Bible tells people who love Jesus to group themselves together. When we work together, Jesus can do His work through us. That is why some people call their churches "the Body of Christ Jesus."

Romans 12:3-8; Ephesians 1:22; 4:11-12; 5:29-32

   The Bible says that each person in the
church is like a part of the body. And Jesus is
the head. Of course, we don't look like
an arm or a foot or an ear. The Bible means
that we all do different kinds of work, but each
of us tries to do his job the way Jesus would.

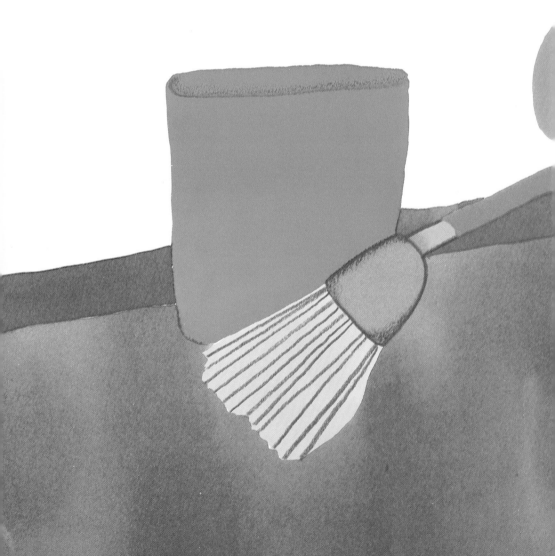

Matthew 25:31-40

In our church, Dr. Yung runs a well-baby clinic once a month so that poor people can bring babies for free checkups. He gives free medicine to those who are sick. Dr. Yung is like a hand.

Ephesians 5:19-20

Mrs. Krem plays the piano every Sunday. She helps us praise God by singing together. She even comes early to help the children sing. I like Mrs. Krem. She is like an ear.

Ephesians 4:32

Mr. Hills seems to love everybody. Once a boy in my class felt sad. Mr. Hills sat next to him and put his arm around him. Mr. Hills always seems to notice when someone is especially sad or especially happy. He is like a heart.

1 Corinthians 12:27-28; 1 Timothy 5:3

Mr. Winter can fix anything. He spent
a whole week fixing Widow Free's roof so that
it wouldn't leak, and he always helps people
move. Mr. Winter is like a strong arm.

Acts 1:8; Romans 10:14-15

The Hakes are a missionary family. They
travel to Mexico and live with a tribe of
Indians. In Mexico, they take care of
the Indians who are sick, teach Indians
to read, and tell them about Jesus. The
Hakes are like feet.

2 Timothy 3:16-17

My daddy teaches a class of grown-ups
in our church. He helps people discover things
in the Bible that they never knew before.
My daddy is like a mouth.

2 Thessalonians 3:10

I work too. After each church service I empty the trash baskets. And I helped Mom carry food to the Green family when they were sick. I guess I'm like sturdy legs.

Psalm 133:1-3; James 5:13-20

Jesus helped the people around Him—
even those He didn't know. But He also took
care of His friends. He expects people in
His church to take care of each other too.
The Bible says we should sing together.
We should share the good things that happen
to us. We should help each other when we
are sick or in trouble. We should pray
for each other. And we should warn each
other not to do wrong.

Mark 10:13-16

Jesus also took time for children. Even when His friends were too busy, Jesus took children on His lap. He told His friends that they should take time for children too —that they should teach the children to know God. I'm glad, because I like being part of the church.

Matthew 18:1-6

Grown-ups in our church tell us stories
from the Bible and teach us what God says is
right and wrong.

The children in our church already
do some of God's work. We save money to
help missionaries. Last year, we cut out
pictures and made a scrapbook so the Hakes
could use it to teach Indian children.
When my friend Bobby was sick, we took
turns bringing him a small toy each day so
that he could play with it in bed.

But our church is not perfect, and neither is anyone in it. I'm not perfect either. Sometimes children fight. Once I hit Bobby so hard that his nose bled. Sometimes grown-ups make each other sad or angry.

Matthew 5:23-24; 18:15-17; Galatians 6:1-2

But the Bible says that since we are all in God's family, we are like brothers and sisters. If someone hurts us, we should be quick to forgive. If we hurt someone else, we should stop everything and say, "I'm sorry." Then be sure we are friends again. If someone does wrong, we should show him his mistake and help him do better.

I told Bobby I was sorry. Then we played together all afternoon.

Ephesians 3:20-21; Revelation 21:1-4

One of the best things about my church is that it will never end. Of course the people will die someday. Even the building will get old and crumble and fall down. But the people who love Jesus will live together in heaven. In heaven we will know all the other people who have given themselves to Jesus from all the other churches in the whole world. Even those churches that began in Jesus' time and even those people who haven't been born yet. We will all live together with Jesus in heaven. And heaven is forever.

John 10:16

The church is a building. But it is more than a building. The church is the people who worship God there. But the church is even more than that. The church is all the people in the world who love Jesus.

I like my church.